Author:
Myles Rutherford



Artwork by: Kendall Crute

# THE BAPTISM OF THE HOLY SPIRIT

MYLES RUTHERFORD

# TABLE OF CONTENTS

# DEDICATION

I would like to dedicate this book to my wonderful and unwavering family. DeLana, Brooklyn, Lyncoln, and Kendall. Thank you for following the heart of God and keeping Him first. Every transition and change, every mountain and valley, you all are and have been such an inspiration to the driving force in my life. I am grateful that you choose to be Spirit-led in everything you do for Him.

DeLana, you are my love and my life. I am so thankful God put us together. You have unfeigned faith. You inspire me in so many ways. You are one of the greatest and most powerful Spirit filled people I know. You also are my best friend! I cherish you and love you.

# INTRODUCTION

I wanted to write this mini book because of a strong need that I see is happening. People are receiving salvation through Jesus, which is wonderful, however not being told about what Jesus said belongs to them. For too long, much of the modern day church has "back-doored" talking about the power of the baptism of the Holy Spirit. We have moved away from teaching this incredible yet mysterious empowerment. This experience from God is an amazing and powerful endowment to God's people. Jesus even said, it was to our "advantage" that He died so that we could receive this wonderful experience.

This generation is hungry! I am seeing a "turning towards" the things of God. People are feeling that there is more to this Christian walk. They are looking for a supernatural touch of God. They are looking for the baptism of the Holy Spirit. Maybe that is why you are reading this.

I want this book to give you a quick understanding on this subject. Then, in the last chapter, I tell you how to receive this wonderful gift. Get ready to be used by God in a powerful way. I believe that your life will be forever changed.

Myles Rutherford
MylesandDeLana.com

# CHAPTER 1

# THE HOLY SPIRIT AND WHO HE IS TO YOU

Genesis in the Bible translates "beginnings." The very first chapter in verses 1 and 2, the Bible says,

> *Genesis 1:1-2*
> *In the beginning God created the heavens and the earth. The earth was without form and void; and darkness was on the face of the deep. And the SPIRIT OF GOD was hovering over the face of the waters.*

The Holy Spirit has been moving since day one! The word for HOLY SPIRIT is "RUACH", meaning BREATHE or BREATH. The first characteristic we see of the Holy Spirit is that He is "hovering." That word means "brood, flutter and resting over". The next event that happens is "THEN GOD SAID."

# RESTS. READY. RELEASE.

What does that mean for you? He, the Holy Spirit, from day one:

1. **Rests** over the darkness and was not affected by it.
2. **Makes ready** the earth for the voice of God.
3. **Releases** God's power to supernaturally create.

This is exactly what He does for you:

1. His first role in your life is that He is not affected (**rests**) by ANY darkness going on in your life.
2. He prepares you (**makes ready**) through a word called "conviction."
3. He **releases** God's voice in your life and changes you supernaturally.

## RESTS:

There is only one thing you can do to NOT BE a candidate to receive the Holy Spirit — DENY JESUS. But as long as you're living you have grace to change that decision. Since the Holy Spirit is God, He cannot touch anything unclean. In order for Him to have LEGAL ACCESS to a person, a person must be made clean and that happens through **confessing your sins**, and **confessing that Jesus Christ is the Lord** of your life. Jesus' sacrifice makes us clean from our unrighteousness.

> According to the Bible:
> *1 John 1:9, If we confess our sins, he is faithful and just to forgive us our sins, and to cleanse us from all unrighteousness.*

> *Romans 10:9, That if you confess with your mouth the Lord Jesus and believe in your heart that God has raised Him from the dead, you will be saved.*

The moment you do that, He, the Holy Spirit, has legal access into your life to "make ready and release." You can be filled with the Holy Spirit. However, the BAPTISM of the Holy Spirit comes after this. We will get to that shortly!

## MAKE READY:

This part can be as long as you make it to be. Some people go their whole lives being filled with God's Spirit but never allow Him to be released through the baptism of the Holy Spirit. The Bible says that after Jesus was raised from the dead, He then did something. He BREATHED on them and said "receive the Holy Spirit." Just like in Genesis, the Holy Spirit is RUACH meaning breath of God. Jesus is the Lord of all and Jesus breathes on the people.

> **You can have all of heaven in you and NEVER RELEASE IT.**

Then Jesus taught them for 40 days and commanded them to wait for the PROMISE of the Father (the Holy Spirit). They have the Holy Spirit in them, but then Jesus says wait for the Holy Spirit — seems confusing, but it's not, when you realize that having the Holy Spirit and the Holy Spirit having you are two different MOMENTS in your life. That is another chapter — keep reading.

*John 20:22*
*And when He had said this, He breathed on them, and said to them, “Receive the Holy Spirit”.*

*Acts 1:1-5*
*The former treatise have I made, O Theophilus, of all that Jesus began both to do and teach, until the day in which he was taken up, after that he through the Holy Ghost had given commandments unto the apostles whom he had chosen: To whom also he shewed himself alive after his passion by many infallible proofs, being seen of them forty days, and speaking of the things pertaining to the kingdom of God: And, being assembled together with them, commanded them that they*

*should not depart from Jerusalem, but* ***wait for the promise of the Father,*** *which, saith he, ye have heard of me. For John truly baptized with water; but* ***ye shall be baptized with the Holy Ghost*** *not many days hence.*

Just like in Genesis, the Holy Spirit was on the earth, making ready for the voice of God to work supernaturally. So is the same when you confess Jesus as your Lord and you receive the Holy Spirit. You can have all of heaven in you and never RELEASE IT. Jesus told them to go and wait for THE PROMISE. He said this is what will happen when you are baptized in the Holy Spirit:

*Acts 1:8*
*But ye shall receive power, after that the Holy Ghost is come*

*upon you: and ye shall be witnesses unto me both in Jerusalem, and in all Judaea, and in Samaria, and unto the uttermost part of the earth.*

## RELEASE:

Remember in Genesis, that the Holy Spirit was on the face of the earth, but God's voice had not yet come or changed anything? There was no supernatural release of light. There was no life, no movement, everything was just waiting! Sounds like a lot of people after they get saved. They think that's it. They sit still, have no life, and die. But that's not it! There is MORE! If you confessing Christ was to ONLY get you to heaven, WHY DIDN'T YOU DROP DEAD IMMEDIATELY AFTER YOU CONFESSED?

God called you to MORE than just going from earth to heaven — He called you to bring heaven to earth! God gave us a promise —THE PROMISE. That promise allows us to operate in power. The scripture above says we will RECEIVE POWER after the Holy Ghost is on us, and next, be His witness on the earth! You are filled with the baptism of the Holy Spirit to release God's voice on the earth WITH POWER! You are not to live a pretty little life with no excitement, no passion, a bunch of rules and regulations that keep you feeling as if you can't add up. NO! You have the

**God called you to MORE than just going from earth to heaven... He called you to bring heaven to earth!**

PROMISE! Release it! What does that look like, sound like, feel like? Keep reading.

# CHAPTER 2

# HAVING THE HOLY SPIRIT VERSES THE HOLY SPIRIT HAVING YOU

# LEAD LIKE JESUS

The first four books of the New Testament are Matthew, Mark, Luke and John. These are called "The Gospels" of Jesus Christ. It's like a small set of books inside the Bible of four different accounts of Jesus. It tells of Jesus and His disciples during the time Jesus was being born to His resurrection and ascension back to heaven. Then the New Testament goes to the book of Acts. This is where things change for the disciples and that is what I want to focus on to show you something.

These disciples were "followers" of Christ in the four gospels. But in Acts something changed in them that made them go from followers to leaders. Something happened that changed their boldness. They were full of faith and full of God. They went from BEING LED BY JESUS TO LEADING LIKE JESUS. What happened? Simple. They received the BAPTISM OF THE HOLY SPIRIT.

> *Acts 2:1, When the Day of Pentecost had fully come, they were all with one accord in one place. And suddenly there came a sound from heaven, as of a rushing mighty wind, and it filled the whole house where they were sitting. Then there appeared to them divided tongues, as of fire, and one sat upon each of them. And they were all filled with the Holy Spirit and began to speak with other tongues, as the Spirit gave them utterance.*

They received the promise of the Father. The Holy Spirit came on them but this time, IN THEM! They were FILLED with the Holy Spirit. Have you ever been filled? That means you are FULL! Most Christians stop at salvation. They receive the Holy Spirit but never receive the baptism of the Holy Spirit. Let me give you this illustration to explain further why you need the baptism of the Holy Spirit.

**Go from being led by Jesus to leading like Jesus**

A man is walking on the beach on a hot summer day carrying a bottle of water. He opens that bottle of water and takes a sip of it as he pleases. He gets a small refreshing and temporary relief. He looks at the ocean over and over as he is walking beside it. He decides to get in the water. All the sudden he is totally submerged and the water is carrying him. He is FULLY refreshed. What is the difference? At one point he was carrying the water, but now the water is carrying him! THAT'S THE DIFFERENCE THAT THE BAPTISM OF THE HOLY SPIRIT MAKES ON THE BELIEVER.

How many times have you felt like there has to be more? Well there is! God didn't die for you to take a sip of Him one or two times a week. No. He died that you could jump in and have the same PROMISE that He had. At one point Jesus said, it is "EXPEDIENT" that I die — it is to your "ADVANTAGE" that I go away (die and resurrect).

*John 16:5-7, But now I go away to Him who sent Me, and none of you asks Me, 'Where are You going?' But because I have said these things to you, sorrow has filled your heart. Nevertheless I tell you the truth.* ***<u>It is to your advantage</u>*** *that I go away; for if I do not go away, the Helper will not come to you; but if I depart, I will send Him to you.*

That is what happened to the disciples. They were ordinary men just like you and I. But when they were baptized in the Holy Spirit, they became led by the Holy Spirit, just like Jesus. They went from being led by Jesus to leading like Jesus.

I love this quote from Myles Munroe, "A lot of people preach Jesus but they don't preach what Jesus preached". That is the Kingdom. It's the OCEAN we just talked about! Operating from a different place than your flesh. Operating by being led with the Holy

Spirit. People know ABOUT the Holy Spirit but Jesus died for you to KNOW the Holy Spirit. It's relational.

That ocean we keep talking about can be intimidating to someone who never swims. Many people are afraid of swimming but the truth is they don't know how to swim. Once they learn how to swim, they are ready to go to the pool every chance they get. They think, "I wish I would have learned how to swim a long time ago." EVERYONE CAN SWIM! This book is written to tell you that you can swim. You just have to get in and start swimming!

OH HOW JESUS WANTS YOU TO WALK IN THE FULLNESS OF WHAT HE DIED FOR YOU TO HAVE! You are called to so much more than just getting saved and sitting. Salvation is just the beginning. You are called to serve — to swim! You are called to operate in the same power that Jesus had while He was on this earth as a man. Don't just drink, dive in! Let the Holy Spirit lead you. If you are more than thirsty — keep reading! At the end of this book is a prayer and direction to receive the baptism of the Holy Spirit. Get fully submerged!

**People know ABOUT the Holy Spirit but Jesus died for you to KNOW the Holy Spirit**

# CHAPTER 3

# IS THE BAPTISM OF THE HOLY SPIRIT NECESSARY?

Jesus, the son of God, the savior of the world, had no recorded miracles accompany His ministry before the baptism of water and the Holy Spirit "descending" on Him like a dove.

> *Matthew 3:16, As soon as Jesus was baptized, He went up out of the water. Suddenly the heavens were opened, and he saw the Spirit of God descending like a dove and resting on Him.*

If Jesus, our Lord and Savior, who is God that became "flesh and dwelt among us" waited for the Holy Spirit to "visibly" rest on Him to perform the will of His Father, then I think it is worth us looking for the promise as well. Notice what happens immediately after we see Jesus having the the Holy Spirit rest on him — He is "LED BY THE SPIRIT."

*Matthew 4:1, Then Jesus was led by the Spirit into the wilderness to be tempted by the devil.*

*Luke 4:1, And Jesus, being FILLED WITH THE SPIRIT, returned from the Jordan and was led by the Spirit into the wilderness.*

Satan's biggest lie to the believer is that you stay saved but don't get weird. Satan has done very well in limiting the believer. The Holy Spirit gives access to the believer to operate the same way Jesus did. Before Jesus was baptized in water, the Bible says that Jesus spoke and the people were astonished. After the baptism of water and the descending of the Holy Spirit, they said Jesus spoke with authority and amazed the people. I would rather speak with authority than to speak to astonish you.

The Bible says in the above scripture reference, Luke 4:1 that Jesus was FILLED. That word "FILLED" in the Bible means "furnished to accomplish and fully supply." Think of how that relates to you.

The Bible says you are a temple of the Holy Spirit.

> *1 Corinthians 6:19,* Do you not know that your body is the temple of the Holy Spirit who is in you?

To be filled, means fully furnished. God gives your house full furnishings. I find that many people are satisfied having a new house (salvation) but having no furnishings (baptism of the Holy Spirit).

A fully furnished house means you bring nothing to the new house. It's all there! All you need is there! You just come in and occupy!

The Holy Spirit comes into the believer and seals them to go to heaven! But the baptism of the Holy Spirit brings heaven down to earth while they are here! Heaven's house address on earth is YOU. And God wants heaven to invade earth. If salvation's purpose was ONLY to get you to heaven, then why don't you just drop dead immediately after salvation? Because God has a powerful purpose on earth for you to accomplish! You NEED the baptism of the Holy Spirit just like Jesus did.

**The Bible says you are the temple of the Holy Spirit**

Salvation is the first work of grace for every sinner, then after salvation the baptism of the Holy Spirit is the next work of grace. And that happens just like the first one. You simply receive it by faith! I'll explain more in the next chapter.

So is the baptism of the Holy Spirit necessary to get to heaven? NO. Is the baptism of the Holy Spirit necessary to function in heavens power on earth? I would say YES! So many believers are just used to accepting that there is nothing they can do about anything. But the authority and empowerment that comes from the baptism of the Holy Spirit will change your life and the lives of others around you!

The Holy Spirit brings us back into completeness of God when we confess

Jesus is our Lord. The baptism of the Holy Spirit fills us with power to do the will of God on earth.

## ENDUED WITH POWER

The baptism of the Holy Spirit is not simply for our enjoyment, but rather for "endowment."

> *Luke 24:46-49, He said to them, "Thus it is written, and thus it was necessary for the Christ to suffer and to rise from the dead the third day, and that repentance and remission of sins should be preached in His name to all nations, beginning at Jerusalem. And you are witnesses of these things. Behold, I send the Promise of My Father upon you; but tarry in*

*the city of Jerusalem until you are* ***endued*** *with power from on high."*

Did you see that? FIRST, It was necessary that I die and rise from the dead — that repentance should be preached (salvation). SECOND, Behold I send "THE PROMISE OF MY FATHER" upon you — you will be "endued" with POWER! THERE ARE TWO SEPARATE THINGS HAPPENING HERE!

**The baptism of the Holy Spirit is not simply for our enjoyment, but rather for endowment**

The Baptism of the Holy Spirit changes your desire from wanting to be served to becoming a servant. Endued means to "clothe with power." Putting on something that gives you power. This means to serve and not simply to be served. Oh that we would know that FULLNESS that comes from being a servant rather than simply being served. The baptism of the Holy Spirit is not only an emotion...it's an endowment! It is not a parade, it is power. It is for service! Serving God's people and showing off God's power to the people of the world.

There is more! There is so much more for you. The baptism of the Holy Spirit isn't for the weird ones, it's for the wild ones! The ones that will dive deep into the will of God. If Jesus WOULDN'T do ministry without it, you shouldn't either! If you are still hungry — keep reading!

# CHAPTER 4

# AM I QUALIFIED TO RECEIVE THE BAPTISM OF THE HOLY SPIRIT?

There are two things that make you a candidate to receive the baptism of the Holy Spirit and that is confessing Jesus Christ as Lord of your life and having a HUNGER AND THIRST for it. Believing and receiving that His blood shed for you on the cross has cleansed you from all unrighteousness. When that confession and belief is rooted in you, you are now cleaned by the power of His sacrifice.

## Is Jesus your Lord and Savior?

> *Romans 10:9-13, That if you* ***confess with your mouth the Lord Jesus and believe in your heart that God has raised Him from the dead, you will be saved.*** *For with the heart one believes unto righteousness,*

*and with the mouth confession is made unto salvation. For the Scripture says, "Whoever believes on Him will not be put to shame." For there is **no distinction between Jew and Greek, for the same Lord over all is rich to all who call upon Him. For "whoever calls on the name of the Lord shall be saved."***

The book of Acts in the Bible is an amazing book to understand the baptism of the Holy Spirit. It is the first outpouring of the baptism of the Holy Spirit after Jesus has ascended to the right hand of the Father. Jesus tells His disciples to WAIT for THE PROMISE of the Father.

*Acts 1:4-8, And being assembled together*

*with them, He commanded them not to depart from Jerusalem, but to wait for the Promise of the Father, "which," He said, "you have heard from Me; for John truly baptized with water, but* ***<u>you shall be baptized with the Holy Spirit</u>*** *not many days from now." Therefore, when they had come together, they asked Him, saying, "Lord, will You at this time restore the kingdom to Israel?" And He said to them, "It is not for you to know times or seasons which the Father has put in His own authority. But* ***<u>you shall receive power when the Holy Spirit has come upon you;</u>*** *and you shall be witnesses to Me in Jerusalem, and in all Judea and Samaria, and to the end of the earth".*

Who was He telling that to? Well, for one, Peter was in the room. Peter was a loud mouth fisherman and hot tempered. Peter had just denied Christ three times during the season where Jesus was being crucified. Yet Jesus speaks to him about this as well. Why? Peter was restored by Jesus three times in John 21:15. Peter failed miserably yet Jesus used him greatly! It seems to me that Jesus is willing to baptize people more than people are willing to be baptized by Him. We sometimes think it is our good deeds that make us a candidate. Or sometimes we think we are not worthy to RECEIVE that because that is reserved for the "ELITE" in church that have it all together. I can assure you, none of us have it all together. Because of Jesus, Peter was restored and made a candidate for the baptism of the Holy Spirit.

God takes ordinary people and makes them extraordinary for Him!
Now, the first time that the baptism of the Holy Spirit was poured out, PETER, of all people began to preach immediately. Here is what he said:

> *Acts 2:17, And it shall come to pass in the last days, says God, That I will pour out of My Spirit on all flesh...*

ALL flesh! All of us! No one was elite, not one of us! ALL are candidates to receive the BAPTISM OF THE HOLY SPIRIT.

## Are you HUNGRY AND THIRSTY?

The desire to be baptized in the Holy Spirit is the key! Jesus said a few things while on the earth about this.

> *John 7:37-39, On the last day, that great day of the feast, Jesus stood and cried out, saying, "**If anyone thirsts, let him come to Me and drink.** He who believes in Me, as the Scripture has said, out of his heart will flow rivers of living water." But this He spoke concerning the Spirit, whom those believing in Him would receive; for the Holy Spirit was not yet given, because Jesus was not yet glorified.*

Jesus was not yet glorified! This means that after Jesus was glorified He would be given the baptism of the Holy Spirit too. When He said this there were

1000's of people taking part in a ceremony concerning carrying water that spoke of the promise of latter rain (for crops) yet Jesus talked about a spiritual rain coming! A "pouring out."

**God takes ordinary people and makes them extraordinary for Him.**

Listen! The drinks are on the house, but you have to have the DESIRE to drink! I find that people that are dehydrated THIRST! Are you thirsty? Are you in a place where you KNOW you love Jesus but there has to be more? If so — KEEP READING! When the baptism of the Holy Spirit is on you, you will operate in power and be a witness. Think of it like this.

There is a shiny new car outside. It's yours. You hold the keys. It has a full tank of gas but it is just sitting there! You have to go put the keys in the car and start that thing. If you don't, you will be sitting in it going nowhere. Let's try another example. You have all the ingredients laid out in front of you to cook a meal. Everything is there but there is no fire on the stove. The gas is hooked up! But no one has lit the stove! You can't prepare the meal UNTIL the FIRE GETS GOING! That is what the BAPTISM OF THE HOLY SPIRIT DOES IN YOUR LIFE! IT LIGHTS A FIRE!

YOU ARE QUALIFIED! YOU ARE QUALIFIED BECAUSE OF THE BLOOD OF JESUS AND A DESIRE TO BE BAPTIZED. Keep reading!

# CHAPTER 5

# WHAT DOES "SPEAKING IN TONGUES" MEAN?

I am excited that you have made it this far! You are most definitely interested in being baptized in the Holy Spirit. But you may have questions about if tongues are NECESSARY and I want to answer that through scripture.

In the Old Testament, God spoke through the prophet Isaiah that, "With stammering lips and another tongue he will speak to his people", Isaiah 28:11. Isaiah saw a moment in time where God would pour out another language on his people. That would be the gift of the Holy Ghost and people speaking in tongues.

In the New Testament, John the Baptist said in Matthew 3:11 that he baptizes in the water but Jesus would baptize us with the HOLY SPIRIT and FIRE!

If you fast forward to ACTS 2, that is exactly what happened.

*Acts 2:1-4, When the Day of Pentecost had fully come, they were all with one accord in one place. And suddenly there came a sound from heaven, as of a rushing mighty wind, and it filled the whole house where they were sitting. Then there appeared to them* ***divided tongues, as of fire,*** *and one sat upon each of them. And they were all* ***filled with the Holy Spirit and began to speak with other tongues,*** *as the*

*Spirit gave them utterance.*

Wow! Isn't that incredible? The Bible records that all 120 were speaking in other languages as the Spirit gave utterance (the words). They were speaking in an unknown language to them. The Holy Spirit was speaking through them and others heard them and were confused, because the people that were baptized were talking in their individual languages. They were speaking in tongues.

# What are tongues?

Tongues are the language of the Holy Spirit through you and it is completely fine for you to ask God to speak in tongues. Also, there are other gifts that are as powerful to you because of the baptism of the Holy Spirit. The TRUE sign that you are baptized has to do with bearing fruit more so than manifesting gifts. Paul says to DESIRE gifts but pursue fruit. Read chapter 6 for more info on this! Here is what tongues are used for according to the Bible:

**There are four ways that tongues are used in you through the Holy Spirit:**

1. Speaking in other languages unknowingly to you - Acts 2
2. Prayer - Romans 8:26
3. Prophetic gift - 1 Corinthian 14
4. Building of faith - Jude 20

All four ways are in a language that you cannot understand with mental reasoning. Why? Because they come from your Spirit, not your mind. Paul says that when you pray or sing in the Spirit your mind is not fruitful. (Doesn't come from your mind, like natural words do).

> *1 Corinthians 14:14, For if I pray in a tongue, my spirit prays, but my understanding is unfruitful.*

Paul makes it very clear that our mind doesn't produce the words, but the indwelling of the Holy Spirit does. Remember Jesus saying out of your belly will flow rivers of living water? Tongues come from your Spirit which is in you —not from your mind. He is in you. The Bible says Christ (anointing) is in you — the hope of Glory! I think that is amazing. He is not around us, no. He is in us.

> *John 7:38, Whoever believes in me, as the scripture has said, **out of his belly** shall flow rivers of living water!*

Tongues seem to be the dominant gift in the book of Acts that happens when people were baptized. It is a supernatural gift that they received when Jesus baptized them in the Holy Spirit. On another occasion in Acts, they spoke in tongues when the Holy Spirit fell.

> *Acts 19:1-6, And it happened, while Apollos was at Corinth, that Paul, having passed through the upper regions, came to Ephesus. And finding some disciples he said to them,*

> *“Did you receive the Holy Spirit when you believed?” So they said to him, “We have not so much as heard whether there is a Holy Spirit.” And he said to them, “Into what then were you baptized? ”So they said, “Into John’s baptism”. Then Paul said, “John indeed baptized with a baptism of repentance, saying to the people that they should believe on Him who would come after him, that is, on Christ Jesus”. When they heard this, they were baptized in the name of the Lord Jesus. And when Paul had laid hands on them, the Holy Spirit came upon them, and they spoke with tongues and prophesied.*

And on another occasion in Acts 10, Peter said that he and others with him were astonished because the gift of the Holy Spirit was poured out on the Gentiles. Then he goes on to say WHY he KNEW it was the Holy Spirit. "For I heard them speaking with tongues and magnifying God." Acts 10:14 declares that Peter says, "just like it happened to us in the upper room".

> *Acts 10:44-46, While Peter was still speaking these words,* ***the Holy Spirit fell upon all*** *those who heard the word. And those of the circumcision who believed were astonished, as many as came with Peter, because the gift of the Holy Spirit had been poured out on the Gentiles also.* ***For they heard them speak with tongues*** *and magnify God.*

Why are tongues an important part of the baptism of the Holy Spirit?

## It is your heavenly language.

> *1 Corinthians 14:2, For he who speaks in a tongue does not speak to men but to God, for no one understands him; however, in the spirit he speaks mysteries.*

## They build up faith in the believer.

> *Jude 20, But you, beloved, building yourselves up on your most holy faith, praying in the Holy Spirit.*

Maybe you have been in a service where everyone was speaking in tongues. This is why. They are building up faith. Not getting more faith, no — building it up. Engaging the faith that

God has put in you. Speaking in tongues builds up your Spirit to fully operate in the supernatural.

## Tongues are intercession for others ACCORDING to the Will of God:

> *Romans 8:26-27, Likewise the Spirit also helps in our weaknesses. For we do not know what we should pray for as we ought, but the Spirit Himself makes intercession for us with groanings which cannot be uttered. Now He who searches the hearts knows what the mind of the Spirit is, because He makes intercession for the saints according to the will of God.*

This promise is for everyone,
INCLUDING YOU!

> *Acts 2: 38-39, Then Peter said to them, "Repent, and let every one of you be baptized in the name of Jesus Christ for the remission of sins; and you shall receive the gift of the Holy Spirit.* ***For the promise is to you and to your children, and to all who are afar off, as many as the Lord our God will call."***

God didn't leave anyone out —praying in tongues is for everyone who desires. God shows no partiality.

If you want to receive the baptism of the Holy Spirit — KEEP READING. You are almost there! And not only that, but you will have an understanding on what the baptism of the Holy Spirit is and why you need it! KEEP READING!

# CHAPTER 6

# THE FRUIT OF THE HOLY SPIRIT

God has given us a wonderful Helper, His name is the Holy Spirit. He equips the believer with an arsenal of gifts (supernatural power) and fruits (supernatural temperament).

Some would say that in order to know if someone is truly baptized in the Holy Spirit, they would see the gifts in operation only. But that is not entirely true. There are a lot of people that seemingly operate in the gifts the Holy Spirit gives but don't have the fruit. Paul explains the importance of having the fruit. The fruit of a tree is truly determined by what it is connected to. A gift is a gift. That is what it is. But fruit comes from something you are connected to.

| GIFTS (1 CORINTHIANS 12) | FRUITS (GALATIANS 5:22) |
|---|---|
| 1. WORD OF WISDOM | LOVE |
| 2. WORD OF KNOWLEDGE | JOY |
| 3. FAITH | PEACE |
| 4. GIFTS OF HEALING | PATIENCE |
| 5. WORKING OF MIRACLES | GOODNESS |
| 6. PROPHECY | FAITHFULNESS |
| 7. DISCERNING OF SPIRITS | GENTLENESS |
| 8. DIFFERENT KINDS OF TONGUES | KINDNESS |
| 9. INTERPRETATION OF TONGUES | SELF-CONTROL |

While this is not a book to dissect the meanings of each gift and each fruit, I want to point out that God equips you with them. They are supernaturally given. When the Holy Spirit is in operation in your life, you are going to bear these fruits. The gifts of God are to be "DESIRED" and the fruits are to be "PURSUED."

> *1 Corinthians 14:1, Pursue love (fruit) and desire spiritual gifts (gift)*

God knew that we would need the fruit in our lives more than we need the gifts. Thank God for the gifts, but they mean nothing TO US without the fruit. The fruit is more important to us than the gifts. However, THANK YOU GOD FOR THE GIFTS AS WELL! 1 Corinthians 13 covers this well by saying that you can have all the gifts but if you have no love, it means nothing! You can be the biggest prophetic voice in the world, the world's richest philanthropist and giver in church, but if your fruit is not intact, something is wrong. Not only that, the Bible says it PROFITS US nothing! If you can speak in tongues, cast out devils, and prophesy but you can't love your neighbor, or even your enemies, you need to pursue the fruits first.

> *1 Corinthians 13:3 And though I bestow all my goods to feed the poor, and though I give my body to be burned, but have not love, it profits me nothing.*

The greatest indication of the baptism of the Holy Spirit is a life that operates in the fruit of the Spirit. If you have the baptism of the Holy Spirit, it is going to make a huge difference on how you treat others. When you have fellowship with the Holy Spirit, the fruits become stronger in your life. The Bible even says that when we die on this earth, our gifts stop, but love (fruit) doesn't.

> *1 Corinthians 13:8-10, Love never fails. But whether there are prophecies, they will fail; whether there are tongues, they will cease; whether there is knowledge, it will vanish away. For we know in part and we prophesy in part. But when that which is perfect has come, then that which is in part will be done away.*

God desires for you to operate in the gifts AND the fruit. That is why He sent the Holy Spirit to us. It was expedient that He sent Him so that we could access the will of God and have help where we need it. It's hard to love some people before the Holy Spirit is in your life. But when He is in your life, it becomes easier! The fruit of the Spirit are the GODLY ATTRIBUTES that are given to the believer. Thank God for them and ask for the fruit to flow in your life.

# CHAPTER 7

# HOW TO RECEIVE THE BAPTISM OF THE HOLY SPIRIT

STOP! If you have not read the previous chapters, I urge you to go back and read them first. It is so vital to get an understanding on why this powerful baptism is NECESSARY so that you don't have a zeal for it, without knowledge. Sometimes we can skip the important stuff to try and read only what we think is important. This was written to equip you and then empower you. If you have already read the other chapters, you are ready!!

## Have you made Jesus your Lord and Savior?

First off, I want you to understand that this is a gift from God just like salvation. What do you do to receive a gift? You take it! There is nothing else you must do in order to receive this gift. Claim it!

The baptism of the Holy Spirit is given freely after salvation.

Have you confessed Jesus as Lord of your life? If not, do that first! That is the most important thing you can do. Say this prayer from your heart:

> "Father, I thank you for giving your Son, Jesus Christ, as the perfect sacrifice for my sin. I renounce my sin, and I confess Jesus to be Lord of my life. I choose to be obedient to you with my life. I BELIEVE and RECEIVE all that Jesus did, that He died on a cross, was buried in a tomb and then rose on the third day. I confess Him as my Lord and Savior and I am assured that I will spend eternity in heaven. In Jesus' name. Amen."

Now you are ready!

## Receive the Baptism of the Holy Spirit

Just like you received salvation, it is the same way you receive the baptism of the Holy Spirit — by faith! Since the day of Pentecost in Acts 2, there has no longer been a need to "tarry" or "wait." Some still wait but only because there is a preparation that they are experiencing in their heart. Regardless of how long that is or if it is immediate — keep asking! But don't forget to receive it by faith, not your works! Remember this is a gift. You don't work for a gift, you simply receive it!

> *Luke 11:13, If you then, being evil, know how to give good gifts to your children, how much*

> *more will your heavenly Father give the Holy Spirit to **<u>those who ask Him!</u>**"*

Seek the Baptizer rather than the baptism. Jesus is the one who baptizes you! Seek Him and ask Him. He will give the baptism of the Holy Spirit to you!

When you ask for the Holy Spirit, remember that the Holy Spirit will not talk for you, but THROUGH YOU. You must speak! You must take that step of faith and speak out what the Holy Spirit gives you. The Holy Spirit will enable you, but you must speak. The Holy Spirit does not talk FOR you but THROUGH you.

> *Acts 2:4, Then they were all filled with the Holy Spirit and began to speak in different tongues, as the Spirit **<u>enabled them</u>**.*

You must participate in this. This is not an emotion, or a lightning bolt, this is you YIELDING yourself to allow the Holy Spirit to baptize you.

## ASK

Now ask! Ask the Father for the baptism of the Holy Spirit. Here in a moment you are going to pray a prayer. You are going to get in a place to receive. You must be fully persuaded that the baptism of the Holy Spirit is biblical and belongs to the believer! Begin to worship the Lord and ask to be filled with the Holy Spirit. Next shut off your mind! Don't allow your mind to control your words. There will be a spiritual

**The Holy Spirit does not talk FOR you but THROUGH you**

spring (well of water) released in you from your belly. Speak from your belly, not your mind. This means that you will need faith to release the baptism in your life. Most people well up with the gift of tongues, speaking in an unknown language — a heavenly language. Just like you cannot speak English and Spanish at the same time, neither can you speak English and your heavenly language at the same time. Are you ready? Let's go! Pray this and then yield to the Spirit of God welling up inside of you!

**"Jesus, I ask you to baptize me in the Holy Spirit. I believe that the Holy Spirit resides in me and I thank you that He will be fully released in my life. I receive this gift by faith. Holy Spirit, I yield to you and invite you to take over!"**

Now RECEIVE the baptism of the Holy Spirit! Take a moment to be with God and let the Holy Spirit speak THROUGH you, not FOR you. Remember, you have to participate! The baptism of the Holy Spirit comes through participation. When you have received the baptism of the Holy Spirit, we want you to share with us what happened and how you feel. Send us an email to testify@worshipwithwonders.org so that we can rejoice with you!

Now, go forth with **love and power. GO FORTH WITH FRUIT AND THE GIFTS**.

Share with everyone you know ALL that God has done for you and IN YOU! Post it on all social media platforms, tell the world. Be a witness!

If you would like for others to be impacted with this mini book like you have, please consider sponsoring these for others to know about the baptism of the Holy Spirit.

# SCRIPTURES ON THE HOLY SPIRIT

*Acts 2:1-4, When the Day of Pentecost had fully come, they were all with one accord in one place. And suddenly there came a sound from heaven, as of a rushing mighty wind, and it filled the whole house where they were sitting. Then there appeared to them divided tongues, as of fire, and one sat upon each of them. And they were all filled with the Holy Spirit and began to speak with other tongues, as the Spirit gave them utterance.*

*John 14:15-17, If you love me, keep my commandments. I will ask the Father to give you another Helper, to be with you always. He is the Spirit of truth, whom the world cannot receive, because it neither sees him nor recognizes him. But you recognize him, because he lives with you and will be in you.*

*John 14:26, But the Helper, the Holy Spirit, whom the Father will send in my name, will teach you all things and remind you of everything that I have told you.*

*Romans 8:26, In the same way the Spirit also joins to help in our weakness, because we do not know what to pray for as we should, but the Spirit Himself intercedes for us with unspoken groanings.*

*Romans 8:14, For all who are led by God's Spirit are God's children.*

*1 Corinthians 3:16-17, Do you not know that you are God's temple and that God's Spirit lives in you? If someone destroys God's temple, God will destroy him. For God's temple is holy, which is what you are.*

*1 Corinthians 6:19, What? Know ye not that your body is the temple of the Holy Ghost which is in you, which ye have of God, and ye are not your own?*

*2 Corinthians 3:17-18, Now the Lord is the Spirit, and where the Spirit of the Lord is, there is freedom. We all, with unveiled faces, are looking as in a mirror at the glory of the Lord and are being transformed into the same image from glory to glory; this is from the Lord who is the Spirit.*

*Ephesians 4:30, And don't grieve God's Holy Spirit. You were sealed by Him for the day of redemption.*

*John 16:7-11, But in fact, it is best for you that I go away, because if I don't, the Advocate won't come. If I do go away, then I will send him to you. And when he comes, he will convict the world of its sin, and of God's righteousness, and of the coming judgment.*

*Matthew 28:19, Therefore, as you go, disciple people in all nations, baptizing them in the name of the Father, and the Son, and the Holy Spirit.*

*2 Corinthians 13:14, The grace of the Lord Jesus Christ and the love of God and the fellowship of the Holy Spirit be with you all.*

*Galatians 5:22-23, But the fruit of the Spirit is love, joy, peace, patience, kindness, goodness, faithfulness, gentleness, and self-control. Against such things there is no law.*

*Romans 8:9, But you are not controlled by your sinful nature. You are controlled by the Spirit if you have the Spirit of God living in you. (And remember that those who do not have the Spirit of Christ living in them do not belong to him at all).*

*Romans 14:17, For the kingdom of God is not eating and drinking, but righteousness, peace, and joy in the Holy Spirit.*

*Acts 1:8, But you will receive power when the Holy Spirit comes upon you. And you will be my witnesses, telling people about me everywhere–in Jerusalem, throughout Judea, in Samaria, and to the ends of the earth.*

*Acts 1:4-5, And being assembled together with them, He commanded them not to depart from Jerusalem, but to wait for the Promise of the Father, 'which,' He said, 'you have heard from Me; for John truly baptized with water, but you shall be baptized with the Holy Spirit not many days from now.'*

*Matthew 3:11, "I indeed baptize you with water unto repentance, but He who is coming after me is mightier than I, whose sandals I am not worthy to carry. He will baptize you with the Holy Spirit and fire."*

*Acts 2:38, "Then Peter said to them, 'Repent, and let every one of you be baptized in the name of Jesus Christ for the remission of sins; and you shall receive the gift of the Holy Spirit.'*

*Luke 11:13, "If you then, being evil, know how to give good gifts to your children, how much more will your heavenly Father give the Holy Spirit to those who ask Him!*

*Acts 5:32, "And we are His witnesses to these things, and so also is the Holy Spirit whom God has given to those who obey Him."*

*Romans 8:14, For as many as are led by the Spirit of God, these are sons of God. For you did not receive the spirit of bondage again to fear, but you received the Spirit of adoption by whom we cry out, 'Abba, Father.' The Spirit Himself bears witness with our spirit that we are children of God, and if children, then heirs—heirs of God and joint heirs with Christ, if indeed we suffer with Him, that we may also be glorified together.*

*John 14:15-18, "If you love Me, keep My commandments. And I will pray the Father, and He will give you another Helper, that He may abide with you forever—the Spirit of truth, whom the world cannot receive, because it neither sees Him nor knows Him; but you know Him, for He dwells with you and will be in you. I will not leave you orphans; I will come to you.*

*John 15:26, "But when the Helper comes, whom I shall send to you from the Father, the Spirit of truth who proceeds from the Father, He will testify of Me."*

*Luke 12:12, "For the Holy Spirit will teach you in that very hour what you ought to say."*

*1 Thessalonians 5:19, "Do not quench the Spirit."*

*Romans 5:13, "Now may the God of hope fill you with all joy and peace in believing, that you may abound in hope by the power of the Holy Spirit."*

*There are so many more! Get in the word and see for yourself! God is an amazing God and we are not alone!*

Made in the USA
Columbia, SC
15 July 2023

20352348R00055